Grade
K
Ages 5–6

Master Math at Home

Measurement

Scan the QR code to help your child's learning at home.

 | MATH
NO PROBLEM!

mastermathathome.com

How to use this book

Math — No Problem! created **Master Math at Home** to help children develop fluency in the subject and a rich understanding of core concepts.

Key features of the Master Math at Home books include:

- Carefully designed lessons that provide structure, but also allow flexibility in how they're used. For example, some children may want to write numbers, while others might want to trace.

- Speech bubbles containing content designed to spark diverse conversations, with many discussion points that don't have obvious "right" or "wrong" answers.

- Rich illustrations that will guide children to a discussion of shapes and units of measurement, allowing them to make connections to the wider world around them.

- Exercises that allow a flexible approach and can be adapted to suit any child's cognitive or functional ability.

- Clearly laid-out pages that encourage children to practice a range of higher-order skills.

- A community of friendly and relatable characters who introduce each lesson and come along as your child progresses through the series.

You can see more guidance on how to use these books at **mastermathathome.com**.

We're excited to share all the ways you can learn math!

Copyright © 2022 Math — No Problem!

Math — No Problem!
mastermathathome.com
www.mathnoproblem.com
hello@mathnoproblem.com

First American Edition, 2022
Published in the United States by DK Publishing
1745 Broadway, 20th Floor, New York, NY 10019

22 23 24 25 26 10 9 8 7 6 5 4 3 2 1
002–327117–Nov/2022

A catalog record for this book is available from the Library of Congress.

ISBN: 978-0-7440-5176-6
Printed and bound in China

For the curious
www.dk.com

MIX
Paper | Supporting responsible forestry
FSC www.fsc.org   FSC™ C018179

This book was made with Forest Stewardship Council™ certified paper—one small step in DK's commitment to a sustainable future. For more information go to www.dk.com/our-green-pledge

Acknowledgments
The publisher would like to thank the authors and consultants Andy Psarianos, Judy Hornigold, Adam Gifford, Dr. Wong Khoon Yoong, and Dr. Anne Hermanson.

The Castledown typeface has been used with permission from the Colophon Foundry.

Contents

Ruby   Elliott   Amira   Charles   Lulu   Sam   Oak   Holly   Ravi   Emma   Jacob   Hannah

How Many?

How many eggs does each bird have? Who has more?

We can count to find how many.

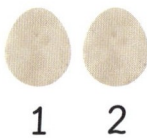

1   2

We can count the brown eggs, too.

1   2   3   4   5

We can match up the eggs to find who has more.

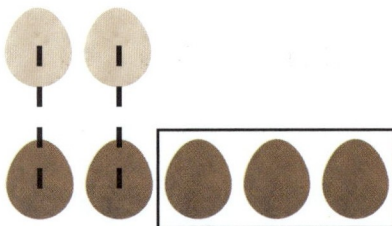

5 eggs is more than 2 eggs.
5 is greater than 2.

2 eggs is fewer than 5 eggs.
2 is less than 5.

1 Count to find how many squirrels. Write the number.

There are ☐ squirrels.

2 Count to find how many acorns. Write the number.

There are ☐ acorns.

3 Match to find which is fewer. Write **more** or **fewer**.

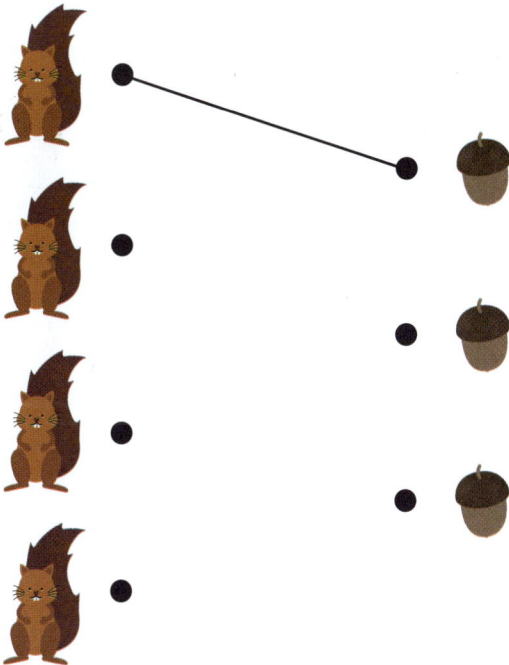

I match
to compare.

There are ☐ squirrels than acorns.

There are ☐ acorns than squirrels.

Sorting by Counting

How can you sort the vehicles?

Example

Bicycles have 2 wheels.

Tricycles have 3 wheels.

We can sort by the number of wheels.

2 wheels

3 wheels

4 wheels

1 Sort.

How did you sort?
I sorted by the number of [ ] .

2 How many of each type of boat are there?

(a) There are [ ] boats with two sails.

(b) There are [ ] boats with three sails.

(c) There are [ ] boats with four sails.

3 Complete the chart.
Put a [✗] to show how many.

✗		
✗		
✗		
✗		

Comparing Two Objects

Starter

How can you compare the sunflowers?

Example

is **tall**.

is **taller**.

We can also compare length.

is **long**.

is **longer**.

1 Compare using **tall** and **taller**.

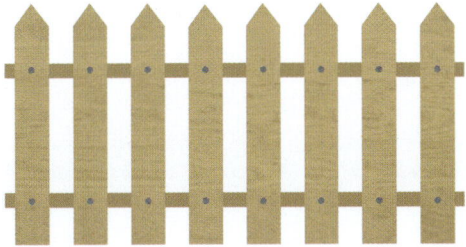

is [ ] .

is [ ] .

2 Compare using **long** and **longer**.

is [ ] .

is [ ] .

3 Find something in your home that is short.
Find something in your home that is shorter.
Fill in the blanks.

[ ] is short.

[ ] is shorter.

Comparing the Heights of Objects

How can we compare the towers?

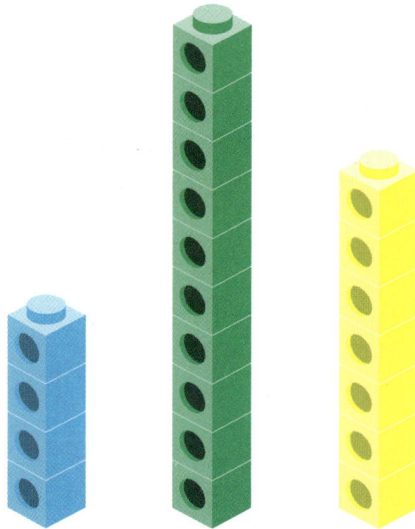

is the **tallest**.

It is **taller** than and .

is the **shortest**.

It is **shorter** than and .

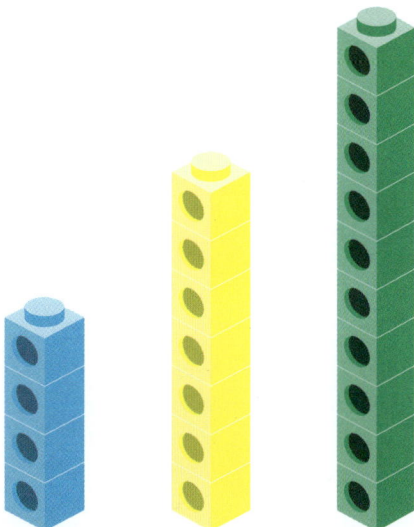

We can put the towers in order from shortest to tallest.

1

A   B   C

(a) Compare the houses using **taller** and **shorter**.

 is [   ] than  .

 is [   ] than  .

(b) Put the houses in order from tallest to shortest.

[   ] , [   ] , [   ]

2

Tree A   Tree B   Tree C   Tree D

Compare the trees using **taller** or **shorter**.

(a) Tree A is [   ] than Tree B.

(b) Tree C is [   ] than Tree A.

(c) Tree B is [   ] than Tree D.

(d) Tree D is [   ] than trees A, B and C.

(e) Tree C is [   ] than trees A, B and D.

Comparing the Lengths of Objects

Starter

Jacob lined up crayons on a page in his book.

How can we compare the crayons?

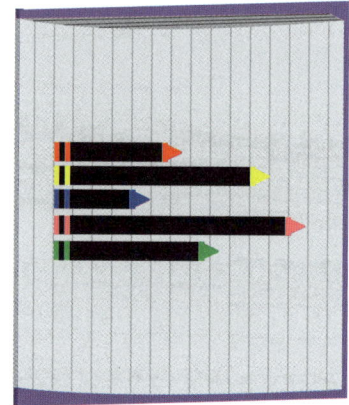

Example

The crayons have different lengths.

is the **longest**.

is the **shortest**.

We can order the crayons from longest to shortest.

The crayons are not all the same length.

Longest means longer than any of the others.

1 Circle the item that is the **longest**.

(a)

(b)

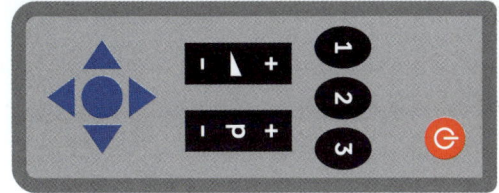

2 Circle the item that is the **shortest**.

(a)

(b)

3 Order the **mints**, the **screw**, and the **watch** from shortest to longest.

shortest ⟶ longest

Using Objects to Measure Length and Height

Starter

We can also compare length.

Example

We can use objects to help us measure.

I am using [ ].

[ ] is about 7 [ ] long.

[ ] is about 5 [ ] long.

[ ] is longer than [ ].

14

We can use objects to measure height.

The soldier is about the same height as four tiles.

Practice

1

Fill in the blanks.

(a) ![orange brush] is about [ ] tiles long.

(b) ![blue brush] is about [ ] tiles long.

(c) ![blue brush] is [ ] than ![orange brush] .

2

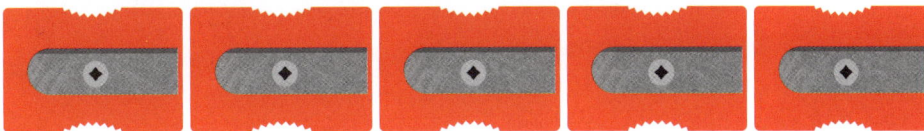

The stapler is about [ ] pencil sharpeners long.

Using Body Parts to Measure Length and Height

Starter

How tall is the plant?

Example

You can measure with hands.
The plant above is about 10 hands tall.

If we use the length of our hand, this plant is about 5 hands tall.

What if we used the length of our hand? Would the plant still be about 10 hands tall?

We can say that one hand is 1 unit of measure.

I am going to use my foot as a unit of measure.

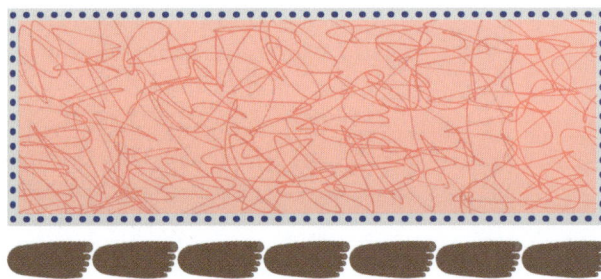

The rug is about the length of 7 feet.
It is about 7 units long.

16

1 Count the 🖐.

The 🪑 is about ⬜ hands tall.

The height of the chair is about ⬜ units.

One 🖐 is 1 unit.

2 Measure your 🛏 using the length of your ✋ as a unit.

My bed is about ⬜ ✋ long.

3 Measure your 🛏 using the length of your 🖐 as a unit.

My bed is about ⬜ 🖐 long.

Using a Ruler to Measure Length and Height

Starter

How long is the pen?

How tall is the mug?

Example

We can use a ruler to measure objects.

The pen measures 10 cm. It is 10 cm long.

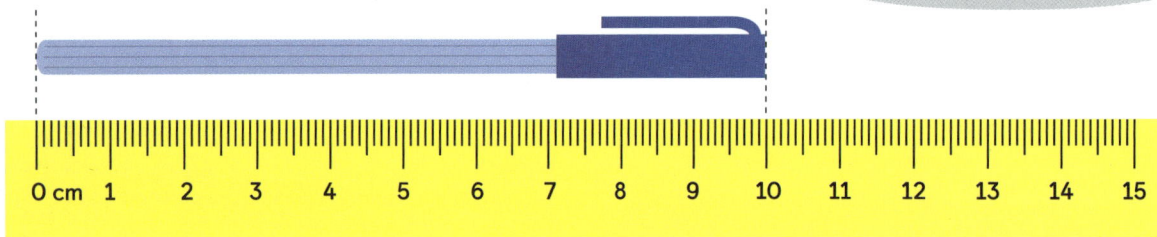

Line up one end of the object with 0 cm on the ruler.

0 cm 1 2 3 4 5 6 7 8 9 10 11 12 13 14 15

The mug measures 8 cm.
It is 8 cm tall.

18

1 Use a ruler to measure these lines in cm.

(a)

[ ] cm

(b)

[ ] cm

(c)

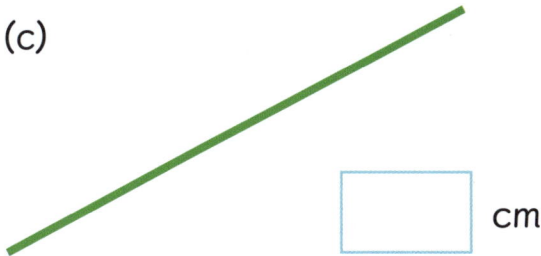

[ ] cm

(d)

[ ] cm

2 Use a ruler to measure the lengths of these objects in cm.

(a)

[ ] cm

(b)

[ ] cm

3 Use a ruler to measure the lengths or heights of some of your favorite toys. Record your results here.

Toy	Length or Height	cm
teddy bear		

Using Next, Before, and After

Starter

Charles is making a sandwich.
How can we describe what he does?

Example

We can use **next**, **before**, and **after** to describe the order of things.

Before Charles makes a sandwich, he washes his hands.

Next, he takes two slices of bread.

Next, he puts the cheese and the tomato onto one slice of bread.

Next, he puts the other slice of bread on top.

After he makes the sandwich, he sits down to eat it.

1 This is what Ravi did yesterday evening.

first	second	third	fourth

played with toys	read a story	watched TV	went to bed

(a) What did Ravi do before he read a story?

(b) What did Ravi do after he watched TV?

(c) Ravi played with his toys at 5 o'clock in the afternoon. What did he do next?

2 Circle the correct words.

(a) Ravi played with his toys **before/after** he watched TV.

(b) Ravi went to bed **after/before** he read a story.

(c) Ravi read a story, then he **watched TV/went to bed**.

Telling Time to the Hour

Starter

What time does the clock show?

Example

This is the minute hand.

This is the hour hand.

The minute hand is longer than the hour hand.

The minute hand shows us the minutes.

The hour hand shows us the hour.

The hour hand is pointing to 2. The minute hand is on 12.

We say it is 2 o'clock.

The time is 2 o'clock.

1 Write the time for each clock.

[   ] o'clock

two o'clock

[   ] o'clock

[   ] o'clock

[   ] o'clock

six o'clock

[   ] o'clock

[   ] o'clock

[   ] o'clock

[   ] o'clock

eleven o'clock

[   ] o'clock

2 Draw the hour and minute hands on the clocks to show each time.

one o'clock

two o'clock

three o'clock

four o'clock

five o'clock

six o'clock

seven o'clock

eight o'clock

nine o'clock

ten o'clock

eleven o'clock

twelve o'clock

Telling Time to the Half Hour

Starter

At what time does Sam go to school?

We say it is half past eight.

Example

The minute hand is pointing to 6. It is half way around the clock face.

The hour hand is between 8 and 9. The hour hand has gone past 8.

The time is half past 8.

24

1 Write the times that these clocks show.

8:30

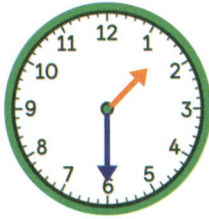

2 Draw the hour and minute hands on the clock faces to show each time.

half past 8

half past 9

half past 12

half past 2

half past 5

half past 6

Months of the Year

Starter

How many months are there in a year?

Calendar 2022

January						
S	M	T	W	T	F	S
						1
2	3	4	5	6	7	8
9	10	11	12	13	14	15
16	17	18	19	20	21	22
23	24	25	26	27	28	29
30	31					

February						
S	M	T	W	T	F	S
		1	2	3	4	5
6	7	8	9	10	11	12
13	14	15	16	17	18	19
20	21	22	23	24	25	26
27	28					

March						
S	M	T	W	T	F	S
		1	2	3	4	5
6	7	8	9	10	11	12
13	14	15	16	17	18	19
20	21	22	23	24	25	26
27	28	29	30	31		

April						
S	M	T	W	T	F	S
					1	2
3	4	5	6	7	8	9
10	11	12	13	14	15	16
17	18	19	20	21	22	23
24	25	26	27	28	29	30

May						
S	M	T	W	T	F	S
1	2	3	4	5	6	7
8	9	10	11	12	13	14
15	16	17	18	19	20	21
22	23	24	25	26	27	28
29	30	31				

June						
S	M	T	W	T	F	S
			1	2	3	4
5	6	7	8	9	10	11
12	13	14	15	16	17	18
19	20	21	22	23	24	25
26	27	28	29	30		

July						
S	M	T	W	T	F	S
					1	2
3	4	5	6	7	8	9
10	11	12	13	14	15	16
17	18	19	20	21	22	23
24	25	26	27	28	29	30
31						

August						
S	M	T	W	T	F	S
	1	2	3	4	5	6
7	8	9	10	11	12	13
14	15	16	17	18	19	20
21	22	23	24	25	26	27
28	29	30	31			

September						
S	M	T	W	T	F	S
				1	2	3
4	5	6	7	8	9	10
11	12	13	14	15	16	17
18	19	20	21	22	23	24
25	26	27	28	29	30	

October						
S	M	T	W	T	F	S
						1
2	3	4	5	6	7	8
9	10	11	12	13	14	15
16	17	18	19	20	21	22
23	24	25	26	27	28	29
30	31					

November						
S	M	T	W	T	F	S
		1	2	3	4	5
6	7	8	9	10	11	12
13	14	15	16	17	18	19
20	21	22	23	24	25	26
27	28	29	30			

December						
S	M	T	W	T	F	S
				1	2	3
4	5	6	7	8	9	10
11	12	13	14	15	16	17
18	19	20	21	22	23	24
25	26	27	28	29	30	31

Example

There are 12 months in a year.

January	February	March	April
May	June	July	August
September	October	November	December

In which month were you born?

There are four seasons in a year.

spring

summer

fall

winter

Spring: March, April, May

Summer: June, July, August

Fall: September, October, November

Winter: December, January, February

In which season were you born?

Practice

Fill in the blanks.

1 [   ] is the first month of the year.

2 There are [   ] months in a year.

3 Fall comes after [   ] and before [   ].

4 The three months of summer are [   ], [   ], and [   ].

5 The month before August is [   ].

6 [   ] is the last month of the year.

Days of the Week

On which days of the week do you go to school?

S	M	T	W	T	F	S
October						
						1
2	3	4	5	6	7	8
9	10	11	12	13	14	15
16	17	18	19	20	21	22
23	24	25	26	27	28	29
30	31					

Example

The days of the week are:
Sunday, Monday, Tuesday, Wednesday, Thursday, Friday, and Saturday.

Saturday and Sunday are the days of the weekend.
We don't go to school on the weekend.

Monday, Tuesday, Wednesday, Thursday, and Friday are called weekdays.
We go to school on weekdays.

Unless we're on vacation!

1 Write the missing words. You can use a calendar to help you.

(a) How many days are there in a week?

(b) Which two days are the weekend?

(c) What day comes after Thursday?

(d) What is the first day of the week?

(e) How many days a week do you go to school?

2 How many weeks are there in February?

February						
S	M	T	W	T	F	S
		1	2	3	4	5
6	7	8	9	10	11	12
13	14	15	16	17	18	19
20	21	22	23	24	25	26
27	28					

3 Do all months have the same number of whole weeks?

Recognizing Coins

Starter

We can use coins to pay for things.
Do you know the value of each of these coins?

Example

These are the different coins we can use to pay for things.
Each coin is worth a different amount.

1 cent

5 cents

10 cents

25 cents

50 cents

1 dollar

The size and shape of a coin does not tell us what it is worth.

1 cent   1 dollar

$ stands for dollar.

$1 is worth 100 cents.

is worth 1 cent.

is worth 1 dollar.

1 Circle all the 5 cent coins.

2 Circle all the 1 dollar coins.

Recognizing Bills

How is Emma paying for her books?

Emma is using a $20 bill.
There are six different bills that we use.

 1 dollar

 5 dollars

 10 dollars

 20 dollars

 50 dollars

 100 dollars

1 Circle all the $5 bills.

2 Which bill is worth the least?

3 Ask an adult in your home if they have a $10 bill or a $20 bill you can look at.

Look at the pictures on the back of the bills. What can you see?

Comparing Volume and Capacity

Starter

How can we describe the amount of water in the bottles?

Example

We can use the word volume to describe how much water each person has.

My bottle is empty. I drank all of my water.

I haven't drunk any of my water yet. My bottle is still full.

I drank some of my water. Now my bottle is half full.

Amira has a larger volume of water than Elliott and Ravi have.
Elliott has a smaller volume of water than Amira has.

Practice

1 Fill in the blanks.

Glass A · Glass B

(a) The volume of water in Glass ☐ is less than the volume of water in Glass ☐.

The volume of water in Glass ☐ is more than the volume of water in Glass ☐.

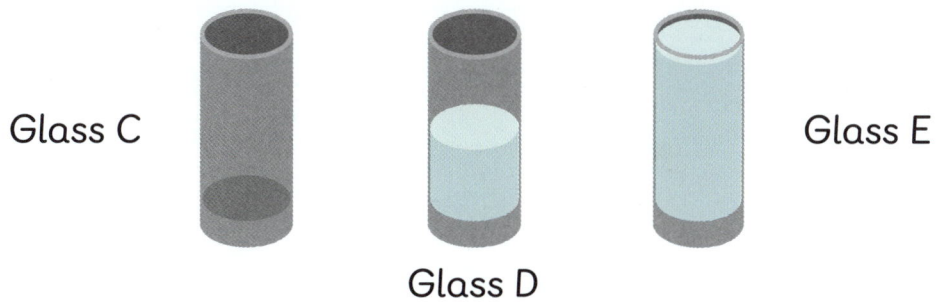

Glass C · Glass D · Glass E

(b) The volume of water in Glass D is more than the volume of water in Glass ☐.

The volume of water in Glass D is less than the volume of water in Glass ☐.

2 Color the glasses to show the correct volume.

Glass A is full.   Glass B is empty.   Glass C is half full.

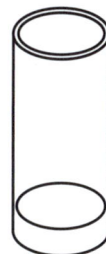

Finding Volume and Capacity

Which container can hold more water?

Example

We can use [cup] as a unit of measure.

It takes 4 [cup] to fill the vase.

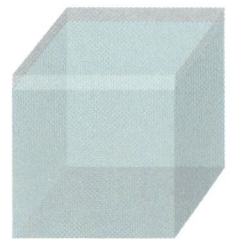

It takes 3 [cup] to fill the water bottle.

Capacity is the most liquid the container can hold.

The vase holds more water.
It has a greater capacity than the water bottle.

1 Fill in the blanks.

The pictures show the number of glasses it takes to fill the containers.

(a)

The capacity of the pitcher is about ☐ glasses.

(b)

The capacity of the dog bowl is about ☐ glasses.

2 Try this at home.

Find containers in your kitchen and measure the capacity of each of them. Count the number of glasses it takes to fill them.

Write your findings below.

Container	Capacity (Number of Glasses)

Comparing the Weights of Objects

Starter

Can you compare the weights of these objects?

Example

I sorted the objects into two groups.

Light Objects	Heavy Objects

We can compare smaller objects using a balance scale.

The pineapple is **heavier** than the paintbrush.
The paintbrush is **lighter** than the pineapple.

The glue sticks and the notebook have the same weight.

1   Describe each of the following using **heavy** or **light**.

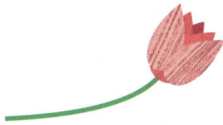

flower

truck

coin

| |

glasses

elephant

pencil

| |

2   Fill in the blanks.

orange   mango

(a) The [   ] is heavier than the [   ] .

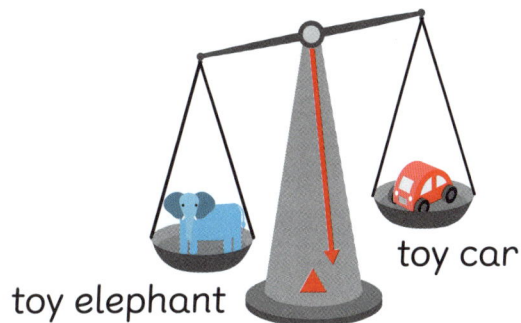

toy elephant   toy car

(b) The [   ] is lighter than the [   ] .

Finding Weight

Starter

How can we find the weight of the fruit?

Example

We can use a balance scale to help us.

The apple has the same weight as 6 cubes.

The weight of the apple is 6 units.

40

Find the weight of each object.

1 ▨ stands for 1 unit.

1

The weight of the banana is about ☐ units.

2

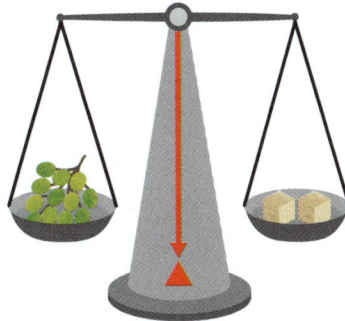

The grapes are the same weight as ☐ ▨.

3

The lemon is the same weight as ☐ ▨.

Review and Challenge

1 Compare the plants using **taller**, **tallest**, **shorter**, or **shortest**.

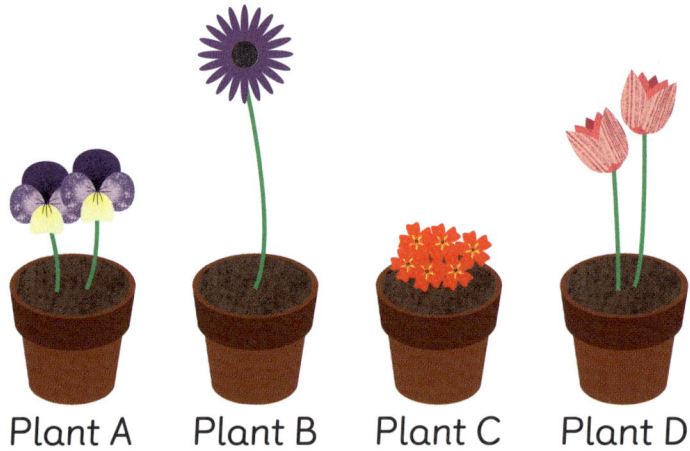

Plant A   Plant B   Plant C   Plant D

(a) Plant C is the [   ] .

(b) Plant B is the [   ] .

(c) Plant A is [   ] than Plant C.

(d) Plant A is [   ] than Plant D.

2 Measure each object using pencil sharpeners.

(a)

Chocolate

The chocolate bar is about [   ] 🔶 long.

(b)

The bookmark is about ☐ 🔲 long.

3 Match the clocks with the correct times.

5 o'clock

11 o'clock

2 o'clock

12 o'clock

4 This is what Elliott does on a Sunday.

  | wakes up |

  | cleans room |

  | plays soccer |

  | goes on a family outing |

(a) What does Elliott do at  ?

(b) What does Elliott do after he wakes up?

(c) What does Elliott do before going on a family outing?

(d) Elliott cleans his room at   .

5 Draw the hands on each clock to show the time.

(a)
2 o'clock

(b)
6 o'clock

(c)
8:30

(d)
half past one

6 Match each group of coins to the correct person.
Holly has the fewest 10 cent coins.
Jacob has the most 1 dollar coins.
Sam has the same number of 50 cent coins as Holly has.

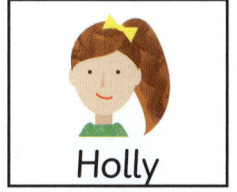

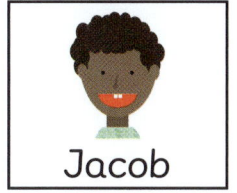

Holly

Jacob

Sam

7 1 🥤 stands for 1 unit.

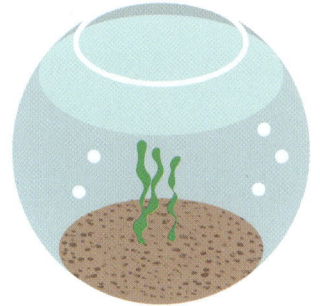

The capacity of the goldfish bowl is [   ] units.

8 1 ▨ stands for 1 unit.

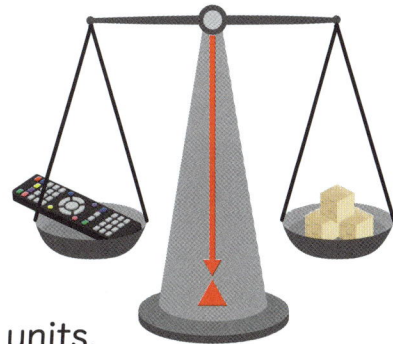

The weight of the remote control is [   ] units.

45

Answers

Page 5 **1** There are 4 squirrels. **2** There are 3 acorns. **3** There are more squirrels than acorns. There are fewer acorns than squirrels.

Page 7 **1** Answers will vary. For example: I sorted by the number of sails. **2 (a)** There are 4 boats with two sails. **(b)** There are 3 boats with three sails. **(c)** There are 2 boats with four sails.

3

Page 9 **1** ▦ is tall. ▦ is taller. **2** ● is long. ● is longer. **3** Answers will vary.

Page 11 **1 (a)** House A is taller than House B. House B is shorter than House C. **(b)** C, A, B
2 (a) Tree A is taller than Tree B. **(b)** Tree C is shorter than Tree A. **(c)** Tree B is shorter than Tree D. **(d)** Tree D is taller than trees A, B and C. **(e)** Tree C is shorter than trees A, B and D.

Page 13 **1 (a)** (screw) **(b)** (mints) **2 (a)** (beads) **(b)** (ruler) **3** screw, mints, watch

Page 15 **1 (a)** The orange paintbrush is about 4 tiles long. **(b)** The blue paintbrush is about 6 tiles long. **(c)** The blue paintbrush is longer than the orange paintbrush. **2** The stapler is about 4 pencil sharpeners long.

Page 17 **1** The chair is about 8 hands tall. The height of the chair is about 8 units. **2** Answers will vary. **3** Answers will vary.

Page 19 **1 (a)** 8 cm **(b)** 2 cm **(c)** 7 cm **(d)** 8 cm **2 (a)** 12 cm **(b)** 3 cm **3** Answers will vary.

Page 21 **1 (a)** He played with some toys. **(b)** He went to bed. **(c)** He read a story.
2 (a) Ravi played with his toys before he watched TV. **(b)** Ravi went to bed after he read a story. **(c)** Ravi read a story, then he watched TV.

Page 23 **1** 1 OR one o'clock, 3 OR three o'clock, 4 OR four o'clock, 5 OR five o'clock, 7 OR seven o'clock, 8 OR eight o'clock, 9 OR nine o'clock, 10 OR ten o'clock, 12 OR twelve o'clock

2

one o'clock   three o'clock   four o'clock   five o'clock   six o'clock

seven o'clock   nine o'clock   ten o'clock   twelve o'clock

Page 25   **1** 10:30, 12:30, 1:30, 4:30, 7:30

2

      half past 9   half past 12   half past 2   half past 5   half past 6

Page 27   **1** January is the first month of the year. **2** There are 12 OR twelve months in a year. **3** Fall comes after summer and before winter. **4** The three months of summer are June, July, and August. **5** The month before August is July. **6** December is the last month of the year.

Page 29   **1 (a)** 7 OR seven **(b)** Saturday, Sunday **(c)** Friday **(d)** Sunday **(e)** 5 OR five **2** 4 OR four **3** Yes

Page 31   **1**    **2**

Page 33   **1**    **2** $5 **3** Answers will vary.

Page 35   **1 (a)** The volume of water in Glass B is less than the volume of water in Glass A. The volume of water in Glass A is more than the volume of water in Glass B. **(b)** The volume of water in Glass D is more than the volume of water in Glass C. The volume of water in Glass D is less than the volume of water in Glass E.

2

Page 37   **1 (a)** The capacity of the pitcher is about 6 glasses. **(b)** The capacity of the dog bowl is about 5 glasses. **2** Answers will vary.

Page 39   **1**

     flower   truck   coin   glasses   elephant   pencil
     light   heavy   light   light   heavy   light

2 (a) The mango is heavier than the orange. **(b)** The toy car is lighter than the toy elephant.

Page 41   **1** The weight of the banana is about 4 units. **2** The grapes are the same weight as 2 ⬛ .

3 The lemon is the same weight as 2 ⬛ .

Page 42   **1 (a)** Plant C is the shortest. **(b)** Plant B is the tallest. **(c)** Plant A is taller than Plant C. **(d)** Plant A is shorter than Plant D. **2 (a)** The chocolate bar is about 5 ▬ long.

Answers continued

Page 43 **(b)** The bookmark is about 7 long.

3

	5 o'clock
	11 o'clock
	2 o'clock
	12 o'clock

Page 44 **4 (a)** plays soccer **(b)** cleans his room **(c)** plays soccer **(d)** Elliott cleans his room at 10:30.

5 (a)   **(b)**   **(c)**   **(d)**

2 o'clock   6 o'clock   8:30   half past one

Page 45 **6**

7 The capacity of the goldfish bowl is 8 units. **8** The weight of the remote control is 3 units.